Hungry Mr. Gator

By Julie McLaughlin

Illustrated by Ann Marie McKay

LEGACY PUBLICATIONS

Special thanks to everyone who believed in and supported
Hungry Mr. Gator, especially Bonny Luthy, Hope Wright, Alan McNeel,
Judith Caulfield, Fran Hawk, Marjory Wentworth, Bambi Werner,
Julie Thould, and, last but not least, our family and friends.

Text © 2005 Julie McLaughlin / Illustration© Ann Marie McKay
The illustrations were done in watercolor.

Library of Congress Control Number: 2005934363
ISBN 0-933101-24-4
Library of Congress Summary: Hungry Mr. Gator is a whimsical counting story for young
children with authentic South Carolina lowcountry animals as characters.

Legacy Publications, 1301 Carolina Street, Greensboro, NC 27401 / www.pacecommunications.com
Printed in Canada by Friesens

We both live on the same neighborhood lake,
where we have had the pleasure of watching the
animals that are in this book. After months
of observation and research, we decided to
write and illustrate this whimsical rhyming
book for young children that portrays some of
the fascinating animals in the South Carolina
lowcountry. This book is dedicated to all young
children, as well as the young at heart.

Julie McLaughlin   Ann Marie McKay

Slinking by the lake without a sound,
Hungry Mr. Gator came creeping around.
Creeping and peeking and sneaking around,
Sneaking around the tupelo tree.

He spied gray goose with her wobbly walk,
Honky honk talk, and wobbly walk.
Sassy gray goose with her wobbly walk,
And he watched as still as could be.

He spied two otters having some fun,
Romping and sliding and wrestling in the sun.
Two frisky otters having some fun,
and he watched as still as could be.

3

He spied three raccoons in a furry clump
Sleeping in their den in an old tree stump.
Three coons snoozing in a cuddly clump,
And he watched as still as could be.

three

4

He spied anhingas on the other side,
Saluting the sun with their wings spread wide.
Four snake birds on the other side,
And he watched as still as could be.

four

5

He spied five turtles sunning on a log,
A hollow log in the wet spongy bog.
Lazy, dazy turtles sunning on a log,
And he watched as still as could be.

five

He spied six ducks with a quack, quack, quack,
Green head mallards with feathers on their backs.
Talky, squawky ducks with a quack, quack, quack,
And he watched as still as could be.

six

seven

He spied seven snakes hanging in the trees,
As they please, in the trees.
Black snaky snakes coiled in the trees,
And he watched as still as could be.

eight

He spied eight frogs jumping in the air,
Who knows where in the air.
Jumpy bumpy frogs leaping in the air,
And he watched as still as could be.

He spied nine egrets roosting in the tree,
An old oak tree, handsomely.
Snowy white egrets roosting in the tree,
And he watched impatiently.

nine

ten

He spied ten fish swimming in a school.
They followed the rule in their school.
Ten tasty fish swimming in a school,
And his jaws opened hungrily.

Hungry Mr. Gator had fish for lunch,
Fish for lunch, tasty fish for lunch.
Crafty Mr. Gator had fish for lunch.
Then he smiled contentedly.

Old Mr. Gator came sneaking around,
Creeping around, peeking around.
Hungry Mr. Gator came slinking around,
But he never once spied me.

Mr. Gator's Glossary

Alligator (al-i-ga-ter): The alligator is a large reptile with sharp teeth and powerful jaws. The alligator looks like a crocodile, but has a shorter, broader snout. It lives in the waters and lowlands of the Southeastern United States. Alligators eat many kinds of small animals that live in or near the water.

Anhinga (an-hing-gah): The anhinga is a fish-eating bird that lives in the waters of the warm regions of the United States. It is sometimes called the "snake bird" because it frequently swims half underwater, with only its head and snakelike neck visible above the surface. Anhingas spread their wings to dry their feathers because they do not have oil glands as ducks do to keep their feathers dry.

Egret (e-gret): The egret belongs to the heron family. Snowy egrets grow to be about 2 feet long and have white feathers. They live near water and use their long, thin bills to feed on fish, frogs, and other water animals. They nest in bushes or trees.

Otter (ot-er): The otter is a member of the weasel family. Otters live close to water and, being expert swimmers and divers, spend much of their time playing in it.

Tupelo (tu-puh-lo): Tupelo trees grow in swampy waters in the Southeast. These trees have large trunks that are swollen at the base. They can grow up to 115 feet tall.